Wax World

WAX WORLD

Robert Mittenthal

CHAX 2011

Versions of these poems previously appeared in Alterra, Birddog, Golden Handcuffs Review, The News, Rhizome, Subtext Annual, Stolen Island Review, W, and in a chapbook from Nomados Press, *Value Unmapped.* My thanks to the editors.

Cover image by Gary Hill, working image from *Still Life.*
Cover and book layout design by Lynn Thompson

ISBN 978 0925904 90 4

Printed in Canada
Chax Press
Tucson AZ

for Lynn

1.1

Skill Set

Today, the usual money vectors as events describe me

This rhetoric describes how failure holds
To rewrite what cannot be renamed

Monday verbs as lunch then snip snip
Day eats at cloud until its tooth clips and records

Tuesday sleeps with cirrus cumulus
And hands off what in sleeveless flight
Corpuscles an engine to styrofoam white

Wednesday's soup alone clouds
What tied together disjuncts
Any shape at all

Tomorrow, animated – shorter, cut off
Darkness all the way back to land
A little image engraved upon it
Shadow of sea – calm a very narrow
Sockets revolving, swollen

Diseconomy of Scale

History is this. Not the same. Which lesson undoes again. So, forget you, forget everything you know. In a minute, given that pause, never slept.

It's all a reflexive dispute – a sort of Big Gulp® – patent pending. Which makes drinking itself – a trademarked plunge.

Infrastructure is such a loss. An internal economy in search of a host. A contingent bleed or parasite in every synthesis.

He was all for show. Dissolved into a point, what will do it again? The premise that French is to German as Frank is to Stein. We go now to remove the monster.

The urge to embrace always returns. Its formula cannot be undone. Full of names, Egypt is the prize. A non sequitur alive in the time of danger.

They called it a street – cobblestones outside, a felt book. 'It' doesn't exist. After great heat, history is this, not the same this. In free books, excess pages. As if – what he said – will do it again.

At impact, a point expanded into a vacuum. Misfortune as good as it gets. What mind over mind yields over time. The formula we cannot be – unreadable collage – analogue of yes.

To posit time pick a number any number & always exceed it. In a minute – until leisure times its opposite, until they never will. Release – an aspect of living against.

Out of commerce, the hors d'oeuvres are all angels. History is this – not the same this. Until yes thanks you.

Unwowed – like wow. Instruments quiet until all rather worked up – until capacity by any other name. Circulating large in the size of it. And capital in its way of exchanging.

My shadow a trap if logic is the same. Whose shadow clear isn't until a cloud was, until the storm will be.

In Curtis's theatre – a policeman sings figures of disgust. The velvet tropes of vaudeville – courtesans of memory under conical hats.

First scene: whose force of innocence sliced into sadness. Second scene: excuse me, I am not like her, very much not alike.

Suddenly dropped, saddled by a listless queen – the mother of all connectors – they altered flight to enter the hive.

Outside, each cell identified drinks. A table is reserved – too internalized to out-think itself. No link to modular estrangement.

Its ceremony is a prison bull. A palimp-form unmasked. We called him architect. They called him a Pekinese. A nest of ifs equal to an integrity plus. A lunatic as the connect – impossible head against a wall.

Specter of these worst words as one gathers disbursements into a bank.

As advertised, rain embraces a building. A transmitter towers words which on their backs present clouds. White, fleeing white. Shadows the very poodles, bulbs for sale.

Silence is in one – whose goals time out. One moment and as moving not. A ticket into a landscape. Shattered as if 1st class.

At last, eyeless in Gaza, they extract an ample remove, the new popular bridge. A congregation of slingshots, rubber bullets. Death unhands what I adore. Absolute negation, unabsorbably yours.

I say 'I' no longer when I see. It – which is it – wishes you – who am I – at work at the million times turning. As big as something ten years later. Remember that a small one is not a short one, and this short one is impossible to hide.

Work poured into a sidewalk. Paper skin in a jar. The heat sink waxed a delinquent barb. Harlequin board games. Ink in a city's street.

Perception by demand quickly becomes an image service. A control to peace – with malcontents. For example, a garbage can in May, brought to you by what gives.

A stain produced value & called in a quality of light. Almost bald, silence – his boisterous swagger whose chores in chortles.

As colorless as the blue mustang, with a vested interest in Rilke. Our featured reader tonight brings sunscreen for the Argonaut. He is the money man. Mr. Mystery with the hootenanny hiccups. A country bum looking to flash. Here to read his money poem.

Until all disconnect, we dished – wishing for it, but only trepanned. Its bullion cubes – to circle negation.

Until disorder eats by acclamation, one stores inflation flavors. In this venue, no argument checks its pencil at the door. White hats and gloves. The eyes, the I's have had it. No circus too tame – until paged, the lessened pause.

Next chapter, paragraph 4: Concerning a magnet, unarranged rays of light. An egregious flock throws up a sponge to content. Distortion's fact held to the fort where the anchor is – where legs, the very patterns, color in a black coat.

So much for physical work. We step through poured walls, rolled into waves. Limbs bob gravely. A wet panic losing grip. It befalls us – the local squat a hammerhead. Flickering invisibility until the dot gain overwhelms.

Trained to lava the brook, it's up to negative use, a sequence of arches captive to the native son. Call him detached – a filament realigned. One snapped to map its grids. The curtain a reject of many.

Time to rein this in. It is worth noting the same silhouettes. Residue a metallic or almost alien capture. Simplicity comes – too late – on the phone, discussing the "as if" of savory association.

Later, more microwaveable flameouts. Dwarf sandwiches for a sportsbar specialist. Lunchable promotions against the notion of a vague or wet kiss. Surf & turf meets sushi & sumo.

In a history of hors d'oeuvres, particles of confetti sit face down – game over. Made awkward, history is a form that re-reads or cannot. Its hypothesis leads to the 'I' we perfectly are not. Many thanks then.

If noses refuse to work, flowers – held stem out. Engines, new windows and cigarettes. Nine months later, an idea is always greater. A story captured or collapsed in a park.

As her talk shows, all acts correspond. Particular chairs are required. Culture couched in a mosh-pit of milder form – where one has always already slept with the enemy.

Attention: Honesty is a methodist who understands. Dual towers a tuning fork – music for a Manichee's moveable feast. The conform is on or up – prayer even striates a tangle.

Buttoned down Brooks Brother seersucker, unnumbered & out of work.

I'm nobody's jellyfish – a generalization I can't improve. Polyester or Polly Anna – that is the question. By extension, in a Cosmo world, fingernails named for someone's mother.

Deserted island folded neatly into kitchen – adjacent to fortress of disposable plates. Let no man eat – a realm of no realms where there is no host. A reflection whose memory – rising column of air.

Come to play with his toy gods, Kissinger on covert funds – was it an affirmative or negative grunt? They played Destroy All Monsters, with Nixon on drums. Error: Improper value – out of range.

Beware: the skin is faster than the word. We experienced the tarmac friendly smell of the faint mechanical. Fifty meters down to split rock, a demonstration of one candle.

Serial commas give pause to the unidentified dog – dancing on the yellow line. The sign said: "This door to remain unlocked during business hours."

His fetish on blind puts, her collar on future lots. Booked reprisals are unallowable, the overhead undone.

Perhaps we pray to be haunted. A simpler yes because plural – but stillness adopts one word at a time – exactly as it happens. Manhattan in one day.

To detour the pain of this condition, imagine the look predominant push to get wherever. The present about face. Bottom feeding at least a principle conceit.

Shelley was right: *we lack the creative faculties to imagine what we know.* This negative island (*each lagoon a lacunae*) means there is no margin for error. A sandbar of separated thought. This is the new kind of perhaps.

He is the self-battering mother of the immediate equation. Uncomfortable in a good way. From foundations cheaper, only a structure fails.

They kiss to taste the time – down slowly. Straight up, dressed in furrows of off-duty hair. Inquisitive, close shorn, he came to fight – a real penknife, snidely living alone with his diaper thank you's.

The footnote said Joyce's laundryman did not really wear lavender flannels. In the tabernacle of tintypes, real values have declined.

Insert an image of thought. Admission of gunshots. Gunshots & so forth. Beauty constrains the famous last. Motorized on uncanny springs, the eyes have it, because detached, one headache over all.

Denomination

Comfort is the new Justice... Naming has replaced class struggle.

-R. Koolhaas

One.

The word 'swan' as a control
Bent plug into the live
A wave form expanse
Flatlines in a backlash

Its virtual is material as material. Dictation for the Cartesian brain.

Zero.

Subsystems of soft – the melting clothes
Drifting away – swirling toward doorways
Indentations hidden from a distance

Nesting in shadow
Carbon threads bent away from view
Invisible frames that test the air

It's a new kind of rupture – euphoria in a tin can
A body gets lost in a trench coat
Draped in black it's fascism without a dictator

Please take once a day with a bit of water
This tablet a sentence of physical thought

Its throbbing walks off – a dream-ache
Soft on the city where
Money elects to flow to the human circuit

A private disjunct as molar – a sliced 2 x 4
My jumble zone caught in a word patch
Where that power to fail to be affected calls back

Each letter a snapshot of what remains – previous occupant unknown
The body decamped, leaving its plastic bivouac
An indistinct wave which yields no magic
No flakes of dead skin. No DNA samples for the imagination

The adrenaline kicks the soft adrift
The erased nose allows everything
Perception jacked direct to spine
The felt pins of a dry shave
Uneven rasp of an evil embrace

The moss welts its soggy skin in the smoldering sun
A tan jello smeared in murky corners

The pulled thread is seamless
A theoretical fetish in film – rubber outside
To explode by example
Shopping for words, vowels presold for the nude – everyday

The secret of not so – if the play house is
'Getting rich' in other words

A euphemism locked in a closet
Its hand over hand as a reversal of vice

Vermont – September 2001

-for P. & B.

Dream is not one – two frames at a time. A pier sitter then mouthing its carbon cue. My charcoals once desperate, twice varied – captured and rubbed in a monks hood.

How grasp the thorny self, every host unwilling. A battery of stuck shadows. For instance Psyche recharged – the after-blast legs. Or shard that remains speaking. A kind of lip synching that rocks down on paper.

To throw out, to throw all out. Packaged attention discards to make up for that person. My restrictions rose. I was tied up in the chair and stood for it. Which should be a verb as a bird in air – the forehead's liquid trace – mist the size of a ship.

We see with the idea that sees through us. Concretions lost in each word. Polished time is the means by which one sees – a hand where the page calls. The remainder are all bodies on the bridge.

Experimental Theology – Connecting Dot

The poetic is the language of the mapless.

-R. Blaser

There are many ways of saying yes
The roundhouse wave, small circlets, the clean and jerky, that sort of abrupt Nixonesque goombye.

Yes in a bedtime story used to dissolve an evening's argument.

Yes in the news retains sensations lost in a storm.
The free association of sailor to wheel. Hail pelted goretex as the ship passes through an eye – lashed to the deck.

Yes to mine.
She sleeps through the hurricane with a practiced negation and dreams in the affirmative.

Yes to concretions shared over time, that is, very slowly.
The furry grips of dew claw. Birding even against sport. Hammers in the song's throat attach fears warble.

Yes whose valley no longer equals temperament.
The fall boast towers – to he who's modeled there, knee deep in water.

Yes as "hello, tree" as direct address to the object.
A performance rather than a representation.

Yes to continual suspension
A text separated from any notion of development.

Yes as a faith is so inexperienced.
Disorganized in strides – who ply right there – to zero out from the depths.

Yes I thought I was stupid
Jealous authority – & I was.

It is thinking motion without a map. Beating oneself up in the dark on the way to coherence.

Yes to the odder river
Careless I a native brook. Once wild a numbness glistens till its light leaps. What years of happy hours sink with tint and bedded sweets. Child with manhood quaking. Planks shut amid fondest sigh – waters rise as its author dies.

1.2

The Assembly Line of C

Whose machine abstracts
Vision's lyric – expression more possessed in itself
When the anima from within fails to project

As alive as a sugar cube
In a horse's mouth

Each reordered word stings
What now for sale is deferred in an internal web
Action's action – deep in the reverb – a reverie

The living corpse is no parasite
Whose discarnate gag is thought
Hold that line, a comedic felony, Hollywood SOS
Where signage communes with the verbs event horizon

Only death, the triumph of Continuity, explains the little c
A kissing cousin whose meaning is an other

Give me bullet points please
Strapped in or tightly coveted
A sort of terrific joy
Partially yours as if contingent or bound to a nest of ifs

We sit beside a tower of bees. A face emerged
Glass polyps – bubbles congealed to an incandescent white
The same torture after 15 years
He swallowed the soap – time's brand in a sterile shirt

Displaced sizzle that keeps on keeping on
More than a dialogue, more than a census or consensus
Manufactured in the quest: an imaginary commons

Diseconomy of Scale

A minor in money.

Majorette cartoon with those fuck you eyes.

Pluralist in red shirt – v-neck to g-string, no sweat.

On a scale of one to ten, the comforts are all determinists.

It's the 'whatever' discipline – finger cots my remote.

Couch potato pie – full of epoxy & resin.

The flicker of game show fixtures – now he's a vowel I'd like to buy.

Caution: Use pause button before elasticity of line breaks.

In fact, every useless poem a stage – green silk top

with Chinese buttons #15.

Please identify.

They identified workers by their torn or bleeding fingers.

This is my facsimile assault – an attack of the likenext.

Titled "The clown of time turned black" or "how

they rank Hegel highly."

Welcome to our surgery – the embrace of the subcutaneous –

a vast bandage to write on.

Today, in the theatre of content, motion denied.

Death came to ride Sarcasm & rode off on the wrong side of the road.

2.1: Draft amendment to third stanza.

Semicolon: no oyster nor pink flesh eaten on the run.

Yes, the body is overrated. Next question?

Tonight's game is chicken in a very expensive club sandwich.

Each collective decision blocks internal difference: Egg-salad please.

It's an illegal combination: body & thing, thing & body –

a prosthetics used to retrain the secular.

A dissertation on what the right hand does not know.

Loss leaders need not apply. Ideology is just their other word for work.

Intermission: Three raccoons cross the road – your joke here – parked

between the wheels of a pickup, lost in the trailing punchline.

This labor is nonscaleable, a demand problem.

She works at that cafe with the free postcards,

inexpressing the expressible.

Time to keep time, 0.2.

The tenured wear t-shirts with the thumbs up sign #26,

parasitic white with an adjunct collar.

Like any successful new technology, each poem must justify

its own existence.

A cartoon economy colored by headache inducing luxuries.

Her new poetry diet reduced consumption of unnecessary pronouns.

In Doug's novel, we continuously say goodbye to words, now unusable.

Briefly banded at the wrists, palms flat, head tucked into a car.

Impairment that failed the test: case dismissed.

Plagiarism as progress. Where now? Who now? When now?

This pain comes not to paraphrase, but to conquer. This pain.

Distressed looks even in terms of inches to the wild ones

over a foot long.

Hooters: whose monster figures these sub-critical facts,

monsters of a single few.

Yellow short sleeved pilgrim with black horizontal stripes #17.

Yet another interpretation of the orange carpet.

It says stuffed or unstuffed, it says look at me.

He died with his boots on – the aroma in error.

This image is itself self-helpless.

Impossible to swallow each pill at a regulated clip.

New gothic single short seeks non-fat double tall.

Giddy as her Godzilla postcard, it's Mothra who's differently abled.

Unable to speak, big hair bowling into it. An integrity flowers.

Whose plural is not; earrings as a sign of former bondage.

Once: we, they. Twice: she, whom, it.

They revert to a round robin – now you're proving it.

Here is the hammer with which to think.

An exile from the land of pillow talk.

Honesty can't even contradictions leash – the public not

smoking any more in.

She said go practice on someone's elseness.

Pretending to be conscious, double agents are the first to fall asleep.

One pulls oneself off to the shoulder for some poetic advice.

"No, officer, a compost of number only wants to persist."

Welcome to my stop word list: cornbelt, enclave, highbrow, lisp.

Lost in the transmission, data from the skin arises –
it is our higher quantity of life.
Small cemetery reveals a sweater, very small cable knit, quite black #12.
When a home is larger than a castle, it ceases to be a home.
B can't see the man. A if disbanded, or B if one can't go on.
High-rise that consists solely of elevators and utility closets.
We swim in a preheated pool, labor congealed around the edges.
Down in the long – his proto-plastic sleep a notch above.
He pressed a ring about the trestle magnitudes –
back to the lowest bend means a wedge.
Translation: you do what you don't want for so long you finally want it.
Its use is a stranger – sheer white nylon with tucks
and rhinestone buttons #33.
In the story removal business, product is a man – if anyone's there.
Go to utilities > lyrical > hexameter.
A vivid wound or a kind of gentler turned into
some sort of plural fool.
The fraction curtains so what – subtle lime green or dirty plaid –
long sleeve #71.
Dear C, I saw U in the wine section. Signed, your fellow in the ship.
Motion censors your majesty, black converse hightop, no number.
These are the veracity schemes: a penciled thread the fiction completes.
Disappearance of anonymous official – black silk pullover #65.
Is that the yellow of nurture or a metallic pool in deep dive.

Appropriate privilege in newly described shirt #1.
Bad example, her person is a simple bridge – catapult
before you found it.
Taller than the Mormon Temple – two towers
keep the greater image across the abyss.
Timed out of life, not parallel nor perpendicular to history.
Within a snapshot of the equivocal, the virtual present arms us.
Profile shadow the smoke rising from your fingers.
Forget bondage – hello content.
Vintage tan rayon long sleeve with white dits #10.
This sentence I am so-called, now taking volunteers.
Hello, this is the FBI, a truck will be in your neighborhood.
Dear Sir, you deserve the thick pile – a sort of carpet gentrification.
Dear Madam, we insert "your sentence here" as an affront.
Help stop feet stop – the pavement not quite on the ground.
Intermission: next up, our elasticity host demands a better boxer.
Action in other words – bouquets – the biggest one with wafers.
If three's company, then two's a crowd.
Sung to the melody of a jerk like me.
Whose knife in hand meets a very comic response –
yours legally for a small fee.
The city word wheel or mayor – blue jean jacket, sweats, and tie #22.
My man Friday – proof that I am not a machine.
Read this. All the amazons I've ever heard.

The thick spires of which or reality central – all owned by the man.
Conflict resolved – a veritable itch replaced by a more
intimate notebook.
Each sentence is booked to die.
Pacified, Mr. Appearance was happy too.
His image of Elvis, faceless – a sort of missionary without position.
A serial code – all geegawed up in total relation.
So that your arbitrary, your plaintiffs, your hand in Vegas,
no longer key to its singular lock – gets down on the upside.
It's like a designer village, or we're idiots at night
who can't see the words for the page.
A celebrated in-appliance, stains in snow, sentenced to
sound satisfaction.
It's the consideration they're after, to wear it proudly.
More mob than men, damaged goods at once more than one.
Or another if he himself goes there.
Refuse harm to expedience – we were – scarcely & widely.
As opposites judge haste as the familiar.
He must – popular and wrong – breed in company.
All little matters I admire.

Wax World

It is my signature block = i.d. comma
whack whack carriage return
lookuptype M underscore

This temporary intrusion
certified as gift – if muscles grow
down into a logic larger

Its beginning separates
            at the neck
so much depends upon a stain

Gravy raised to an illicit power
the necktie invective equal to what black
words leafed out – into a list of hated things

            We wait for the
same stain with a different title
long division of one

A knock out or puzzle
another five-letter word for
we will keep your resume on file

Sweat equity for a finger that
gives them that liquid sign
In other words, reread the credo

and connect the dots. Habit is a streetcar
so named. The inspecific personified
A jigsaw abatement seen from the

privacy of the #28 bus. It is an elimination
you will someday agree. The long acres of fact –
blind man in perpetual close up – moving lips

Labor untied in the 'adjust-me' knot
tops off the tank – an economy of one
or the pigeons – a comic mode of standing up

Until we cannibalize the pride
this cub scout version of events
Hippo slowly submerging – hot swapping

pond items for a swan bite. It's the bubble
disorder in celebration of that ominous
shark sound, ideological free lunch

or the literature that feels good to know you
incest of its most excited theorists
two thumbs up – above the head

but over my dead module
Everything gems its identity of suchness
introducing Frank and Stein on ice

a sort of wurst a la fromage or
carefully flagrant genius – in this difficult
glacier of a book they slept alone

The memory discards again – just call me Frank
there's no such thing as one and one
but they threw the book at me

A paperback or sort of Canadian one-day only sale
lottery now at ten million
but in Jeff's terms 1.47

Wax World

. . . or broken mouth
the something ship

for the photogenic as
modeled by us – call it
Peter Lorre as Raskolnikov

or genetic class loathing
a sort of water torture to do
doing business as: our can-do philosophy

Doing the hee-do
a verb in the hand is
worse – dancing to

the list of a rudderless
or eating to the rhythm
of once a lover was a lover

I was the Dodger fan who lived in a shoe
a Beatnik or food crank at the top of my class
In the arms of someone's other

your joke here no greater than

the very crudest nine to five

in Freudian terms, the big furniture all presold

Wax World

An after-life of merit badges – impersonal apes
in disorganized anterooms. This just in:
X blanks Y, back in 30 seconds

Now serving pillboxes in 18 states, picture
this – gesticular downtime
black and round whites – icing on a Canadian cake

He is the Yul Brunner of bent spoons
a pin straight cowpoke spelt black words
So many hatless sleights whose

visas still require colors
on the inside – a.k.a. white out
and brown down around the edges

We insert your nature here
as if a whole genre is none of that
'above' whose image owns us

For your cooperation – in advance
should you question the foregoing
double that and make like a book

Can't go on ordinary opinion
page turning to figure its own
estrangement – the content insert

you're it! Abrupt equals insolent
equals eat this. A faceless,
unnamed, motion away

In this sentence, my letterhead walks
outside – formally impersonal equal to
sincerely yours

Wax World

She lets the mall speak
a contest of ribbons
ticker taped to a wall

This leaves you young man
Unteachable with
distinguished remarks

Two out of three Seattleites agree
A kind of feudalistic dim sum
or side bursting module

Each stain has a price but
what appears here is not a richness
I have loved but a central

reality agent (bird in mouth)
both secretive & joined
with no motive in verse

A crowd melts – skin crawling in
pinpricks of light. Shadows mortgaged for
words. The beacon narrowcast until the

radio talks back. Unreadable
prisoner a detachable silhouette. He is
my traffic canine – copycat

for large collections only
A footnote or defossilized bird
testing the 19th century walls

Wax World

A violet is a flower one letter at a time
Today's proper noun is National Velvet
My pencil is longer than yours

only means I'm hardly working
Illustrated and indexed, it's form
points to the opening of a mouth

One motions briefly – the highest bidder
at first light, on cue for the business of
amusement. The latchfold is their fluid thing

The familiar reader does not search
but finds. To swallow each number apart
three fingers width – the tongues mud

four frames the width of a candle
Concrete merit in a fashion of faults
The following steps form a grid – or pain & a little sleep

Apart from the purposes of yes
She won the race
Cashed the check and headed in the opposite direction

No portrait of a duck and cover
Belt tightening against such false claims
A landscape explains less as it unfolds

The front of a shelf – the plural of occasion
Not enough hand to mind – a kind of inedible
pun in the truth-seeking missile

100 Words Of Wax

ingrown but active
not listening but half submerged in green

Seawater shadows it
(4) blackberry badge and eyes

this sort of saying names itself
for example, here come the cows!

(21) to sing only & strangely
to name a badge any badge – in sing along mode

no fishkill to tank the still conquering shade
or sour the precious still

whose New Jersey air forgives nothing
(56) groin extended in stiff sleep

the shadows these airmen eat
& pretend to go on

(72) how could they
so refined, prophetic &

still (again) it then is a choice

correction: first song last – sung toward

was it too long the

(98) rain lengthwise

1.3

Gag

. . .indicating first of all something that could be put in your mouth to hinder speech, as well as. . . improvisation meant to compensate for a loss of memory or inability to speak. –G. Agamben

Permission to approach the yellow disk at a distance.

Enclosed in the gesture, a man twists an orange into his mouth.

If appearing not said is lost, memory a speech defect comes with it.
Hand holding hand – no engine of taste forgiveness.

Can't get enough difference – a concrete antenna to balance the sky.
Liar! You glisten beneath narrow cast frequency arrays.

A pun riveted until punched – until its pencil of light cannot be contained. The sculpture says nothing. It harvests only the gray grain & cackles when a crow swallows.

Silence is its stupid thing. A body English out of words – out of names. It fights the flicker of stunted dots – up-screen of erratic paint.

In this school of other import, against the sterile comforts of unbound life, contagion springs a monster. Its original revolt was too jealous – earth flattened in the eccentric threads of that one thing.

We removed the grass, the ants and the words – leaving the percept in a vividness of dirt. Thumbing its green at you – no sweat in relation to time.

A cinema whose separate vacation withheld the steady state. Investigating the awkward between, fact as boundless self-organized. History's order – less the crowd.

At the end blossoms go white – tyrant steam to flame. A copyrighted face on the list of names.

In order of appearance, physical traits empty out – barefoot but fast. It's a euphemism for the poem – a horror of thought. A parade of names scrolled out in the colored lights.

Diseconomy of Scale

I don't understand love, said Charles

It is out – beneath where we can go.

Named before but can't tell – died but don't remember.

Fixed so that the sold or the word since.

Hey Buddy, this sentence doesn't belong here, so move it.

I found the list of a sinking ship: weasel, maggot, immoral cheese.

Is he a Baltimoron, or a mid-career machinist?

Out in Mongolia, he discerned a southern accent.

It's a flag of convenience, management out there on a floppy disk.

No furniture inside, only corporate structure on a laptop.

Random numbers or names on the door.

Goose-bumped in wimp city, they're living it up LTD.

The body English – so forced then – upon a star.

Fortitude that anger in it.

The maiden shell, across the sea, several years ahead of its peers.

We sink below the surface and slip away into the remote.

I had become to myself a vast problem,

hard to grasp, the incredible shrinking man.

Reversible yellow goes over the mountain at yes. A tartan slip #24.

An argument of counts can't even the argument of counts.

Can't stand too much of a good thing, trained

in the horizontal position.

Failure at a rate uncommon – non-stoppable calls – followed by
shift-click, carriage return.
Double short non, with whip – seeks tall drip – room for cream.
An efficiency compartment proved large; in this story
a snake swallows a hedgehog.
Labor equals the connect of is – equals the want to say.
Beige sweater #18 caught in the acid wash – now sea green.
Underbrush, a dinosaur theory comes to malign thought.
They supersized their food chain, and were shortly out of luck.
On a planet scaled to these dimensions, I killed the best of both words.
Until too complex, I can't feel it.
Yet another photographic sequence of someone wearing
all their clothes.
I tailed him and lost myself in the blind spots.
Stan's discursus on the camera angle: identical stories with different
vanishing points.
He drove two cars back to the station.
A body propped there – ran over and back.
Too large for studio windows, the boat in the bottle outgrew its frame.
Negotiating position – two white shirts
unbuttoned on opposite sides of a table.
After 1.3 billion seconds, we figured our net worth = middle age.
After the invasion of the double crust (patent pending),
pizza here no longer tastes different.

To absorb the saturated facts, the lean-to aglow of what pulls –
grave diggers delight.
It may same its seams – ironic and flat.
To outsource "your words here."
Eventually, a body loses its divisions, becoming one.
What was that? Bedsores taylorized in a clinical machine.
Fleur-de-lis towel sewn into sweater #12.
Is it medieval – where everything follows from one thing?
Unsung to listen, subject in a minor key,
reflection that cannot be contained.
He became a no one's "no one" – king of
everything at zero point zero.
Atomized relations entered as a method of containment.
Keeping time – they realized the outside no longer explains the inside.
Luckily, we prefer trees to the forest.
At first, a secret, or assorted soreness.
Soft lead #2, until the buzz in my head equals what.
Yes, in this down time, platinum umbrellas fell to earth.
Handcuffs, chains, an empty safebox.
Yes, Houdini's best trick was the intriguing trace.
Enclosed is your electronic parking ticket.
Compromised – worked to a head – no wrong.
So that overdeveloped words sever what mediated –
as individual – best sellers.

A stream of ink to interrupt the paper futures.

No one noticed until the print runs downfield and scores.

I prefer it. Lonely aisles – nine items or less.

A shimmer almost white as fog crowds anticipation.

Circle K at the opening of the field.

A ball kicked through an uplifting H, next to the bp station.

Well – if not very well – not very well – not.

Left to say her novel is very well. A fixed figure to gender within.

B. lowered case and fired – what? A moebius at D's donut?

After growing down, his affection was not specific.

The evil in ink – black pasta or difficult squid –

promised data on the train he took me to.

Something else cleaned his toilet.

Leveraged as if the language bend was back.

Carpenter of skewed proportion – in a vitrine one foot shy.

Communion wafers written in the mouths of strangers.

Heads up – where too large Christ's body stands a section short.

Each dissolve (signed) in memory of my book; the last few pages of

which are almost blank.

Beauty – a momentum without concept – rides the buoyancy.

Concrete flowers upon whose bricktop walls, trees.

They talked until they reached fertile size.

It is an image disease where one cannot recognize oneself.

His whisper number a symbology.

A catalog of sentences – all below cost.

In the nude economy, a successful poem conceals its business plan.

It began at the impossibility of not speaking.

I hate that I love and vice versa.

Speech implodes in vectors – unexplained.

Identity a simulated bulls eye of wingless signals.

Those angels incapable of being sent or received.

I lived in the empire state where King Kong's rent is in arrears.

He lives in the long run – too big to fail.

So much for Led Zeppelin's greatest hit, condensed

air breeds as the inflated sink.

I arrogate as all planet confusion.

The green bridge at base – soft daddy limp in dark vegetation.

The pronounced bingo of aligned ambition yields – strike that –

a biological escort.

Pass the proper nouns please. Signed all too human.

Like Milton Berle on too much caffeine, distributing

liquid diet headstones.

Purgatives: the whole lot of them first person fixations.

Implicated, we know what transparency is good for.

But lived flat out, a martini party without the candidate powers.

What it is – is his own problem – definition as thankful as alone is.

The cohere already is not – as one's spurs – teeth to hold to.

So difficult is the larger patch, whose laundry scales the cynical seams of a larger garment.

The view perfect bell-hop sings:

    as if groupware for snots

In the boom of Beltway encounters, in a teenage too big.

A vast bandage says welcome to our surgery.

Painful, bruced off – fate underlines nothing.

Palm trees and tigers – the very mastodon

until crooked I – everyone equals

    an era of emergence – equals what under the skin

    as splinters of music divide what opacity plays.

A bubblegum habit is the surfer's choice – unity of impact –

plus suspension.

Priced out of the impossible, each essay obtains word-minus-one,

an arrival from without.

Typeset black: dog to drinking fountain thanks you.

Someone outside this voice reading from a script.

Something called caller ID.

Open space a primary bluff. My hand a show of fists.

He isn't stowed away in little words.

The crow a tower in "yes" or a pigeon within the life of.

I say and I said – galvanized or against out –

headlines the destiny vanish.

Introducing unfinished business, the common

inadequate before it found you.

Each gesture solitary in what refuses. Adopting stranger,
These obvious slogans prove exact. Envelope please.
Passive carrier introduces new postal code. Delivery for Typhoid Mary.
I cleaned myself at the axiomat.
Read a novel of once to learn how these moments,
sequins of doubt, disengage.
Words bleached in the blinds of control. An image scared to be alone.
If there is such a person, turn please a little to your left.
It's my very lips, having words in a cistern.
There would be no war – no words, no cistern.
Complicity & so forth, or the goal between.
Unquantified, he fell out of the almost circle.
A sort of erotics of the fittest or lowball counter attack.
In other words, each mushroom is a specific cloud.
On the bleeding edge, software precedes essence.
But as hard as I try, thinking frogs my c:\drive.
My head is that cloud, not tickling but dormant once.
A precultural agent in lieu of what was.
Presweetened body beaten into words. Stir fry ten minutes.
Such a hive in tractor trailer bliss – compounded later
or separated from myself I withdrew – undone to alarm intention
and flame out.
They leaned into the scrum and teed off.
The letter "N." "P" for please.

It's your hit parade – a predigested simplicity whose terror is wit.

Self service as an engine of amoral use.

A fact forwarded into the blinds I climbed into an illegal dress

(somehow pre-numbered) – into the puzzle picture.

A poetic of card counts: diamonds, clubs.

The surgical forges of cheek.

My ass performs the bawdy windmill dance.

Modesty next level up.

Wavelength

Sincerity is the one great artistic crime.
Insincerity is the second greatest.

–Fernando Pessoa

Michael Snows – wood slats that burr the legs – waxed up. Static a sketch too stationary. Even the eyes of spring refuse the swallow. A crowblack pallet paints our balky night. Who minds a perambulent 'I' whose weeds deform us?

Did I say "burr"? Pungent crisp – pre-cooked even. Odd that over-hopped state locks in a barrel – misdirected as their pen waves him in. Faultless swagger – three star Burnetts gets out of the box. Did I mention the box? Product of Scotland – 100% aged Canadian. Love as such – emptied of its old impertinence. Yours truly, up against blue.

Michael Snows – an April coverlet – Vermont's 70 inches. As if real time could plunge – shot out an exchange – send X's and O's. Looking forward to a mild even luxuriant time. A sudden wet is its canonic valentine.

2.1

Page Up

The meaning is an other – what words are made of.

Access denied to a plagiarism of a sort. The song of the acid washed – DNA minus one.

It's a message heard but never sent & thus not retrievable – the door ajar. A well reasoned doubt. The parallel text wrongly perceived, living with or beside itself.

A flower reprinted on walls until the paper spins. Fingers at indifferent speed. Rationed density in a deployed book. Its larger sheet all to scale.

To renew its request, no one would know. Left behind these impersonal remarks.

A refined sensibility with no aesthetic.

Its centerpiece a hallway that is somehow undefined. I renewed the request, a prayer everyone would know. Names lost on the papers marked personal.

Unlimited incoming, the books will find me. Asleep in the elevator, rising in or falling out.

A dream follows its soft edge as a prick out of water. The boat sank after the ditch. Struggling to swallow the air, gasping to ride the wake.

✲

He is a cookie cutter in a sur-title state
The song drives under the skin
To face up to a landscape
A head of what, without calling back

Between a word and a percept, a provocation
Sound dissolves its surface dance to no longer be there
But provoking itself in the other place
It returns to grasp the spoken

He discovers the main course – the work itself
And yet these parallel texts remain outside – inconsolable
Animal curves that celebrate the disjuncts – crackers
Of comprehension

Toast With Jam®

So here's to Mr. Asphalt of the lyrical persuasion. We singe the bar with his lachrymose brew. Our hand emerged equal – as beauty extracts it, it loses itself in dream – a word vacuum whose images take themselves for a walk.

The sublime order is "to go," that is, lost on or above our head. But Beauty is to touch the broken with all sensation. Sublime is a play to the non-existent or elusive common; it is beyond reach – transitive.

The concrete is a touch at a distance – burnished on the mall, eyes riveted to cold steel. Its folds of flesh broken, celebrated.

Dense muzzle of diction fat. To phrase once – abusive was enough. A near sewage kidnap, ushered in the social complex. A play unfolds under watchlight. Within the prison – wreckage from the walls. Suggestive whispers outside any agent. Fact battered in the drum beat.

Disconnecting Dot – a postscript

Is it a euphoric poetic of disgust
De Sade's eternal return
Sex by numbers – an arched readymade ready to fail

Face paint as if the syndicate smile
Matters
A shotgun mascara of words
Against an arched brow

Half a person please
A freeze frame from the temporary
Whose feet in flats is in the house
To lock in what closed out

Against the false measure of milked applause
An abrupt feel and I do mean flesh
Its scary throb and quiver that stays with one

She swallowed the improper nouns and spit out
The eccentric sky flats. The two-toned anarchy logo
Flattened landscape to supply its own verticality
The ability to expand and reproduce
Unfolding in an inexorable close-up

The earth's revolt – intemperate
Hush puppy abandoned on the plate

She crossed trains to get home
Queen of Verso who erects the
Soft target of tracery doodles
Sewed in an arc – into the arm of a down jacket
Charging up the sidewalk
Head down – finger punching the air

The Virtue of Lotus 1-2-3

Byzantine makeovers, compressed into the fabulous. The skin emerges in revolt. At the intersection of cocktail napkin and ink, the resolution a treasure mapped off. Tied to a lattice, a missing constraint. Strapless compulsion a new sensation.

In celebration of the dumpster's physical facts – an explicative devotion. Fighting the prize – we called them scabs – fresh flesh in each beret.

Shaved and turned inside out. An abnormal opening. Off ramped to seize excess capacity, a functionary or junkie of architectural curves. What gravy lurks to lower activities? Enthusiasm – submerged in flesh, at the memory eyes ingress – the discipline of having seen. Nostalgia a collective bleeding.

They voted yellow, stet that, a fade from green. A copycat's hair triggers a fire risk. The imposing pores of skin, the better the worse it is. In memory of my feelings, crisis management becomes film theory.

Equals a market democracy – redeployed. Their numbers are their names. Each dollar a circular reject – advertising escape. It gathers in pleats. A lens through which – I am some body. Or not.

Can't get enough sucker punched. Endless numbers computed under horse blankets at night. We spread sheets under stars, meteors bathed in the dark arms of our self identical between. Imagine beefcake of the raucous gender. Screwed to a tightened bliss, what dissipation galore, what bonfires slide from an idea of prose.

In the wake of lost potential, the words read us – moving right to left. The singular aftertaste eddies, residing in oscillations of exiled breath. Each title at a time painted the world. We are now a black night of brainwaves – no holds barred.

Hail Caesar

Double pictures no daub will do. To one up adams over & into. In the story removal business – we, she, it. Is for facts a drag. No foundation, no values translate to even the score. Whose feely love from salad days waltzed into a body shoppe – close up to a spectacle of days. A living landscape in the intermediate space.

Clipped, whose crouch, whose lodge of days ice overdue, whose door ajar. No time until memory banks caught in the early lights – staggered into town.

Motion plays to risk its inner lore. The pull cord shadows. An announced state says *nothing*. Unwelcome, life led to nouns, the contained and the container. Remember to bend the knees – one and one and... Instead of tree muscles, closed branches – clarity released. Quiet, hear tinsel in a domain of colored fact – a shimmer in descent. By strange election insult is awake.

A pencil jumps in her hand. A one legged bicyclist with a spare leg. All subcutaneous shiver – dense or external spasms. Her brow arched to reveal: blue, a poem in distress. Equals an animal at war with itself. <u>See</u> outcast below.

2. It's a hardball theatricalism jolts me. The rodeo clown bruised pockets of her thrown chance. That's a tongue – blister assignment – an image fulfilled. Words fast against a wall – against the hokie surreal – phrasal mutation; silence on the floor.

B protests an executive role. It's his cheesecake microscopically. It's a stale, uneven flame, gathered under electric light. No bracket to open lonely arms.

Stupefaction

In terms of revolt, personal expression is the problem. Inexperience dictates the pain in the eye. Likeness a shaft very forgiving, the wilderness a gesture. The word fantastic comes to mind.

Prince of light whose fingers reigned. The piano skin a specimen of muscle. Suffocating warmth in which life becomes king. A velvet bottom to the chore.

The math between them was now barbaric. She saw herself painted – trying to gain a hold, and denied the trophy. The frog & the prince had forgotten how to talk. They danced mouth to mouth until wrinkled, when their bodies fell. Hush! Foreheads balloon into windows. Can't face the step abound. The end a megaphone – that bit between them. Metallic confusion – a belly soft for the stag show.

As is, an object fawns all out of it. To love the closed or adjacent skin displayed as a standing wave. Clerical eddies until the pulse beats.
A family defined against is a strong family. The Quakers subside in waves. They have no interest in exaggerated life. When facts become aged celebrities, the family gets lost. It could happen to you. The iron orchestra sings out. Their complex search is a simple slack – an engine

of sorts. The slip knot admixture requires it. Paid back, or paved over the astonished outside. The blue sky in all its meaning.

Its fist thing – jabbed to annoy – asserted drive to stop – led to cheat the helmet of majestic birds – adjectives aristocratic mistake. Unfurnished prose as the speed of musical chairs – twirling awkward nouns alive to the participle moment.

Obfuscation Deflowered

A celebration of the connects – a specificity in pursuit of
fact is never less than the fiction of a full disconnect.

-a skull & cross-bones for Cecil Taylor

I heap under scored slacks
Edible curves to bell bottom

Unseen bent – no answer
or bent so edible – balanced or not

Isn't the what for –then– now?
His difference a what if – or thick knot expressed to none

So kind – like kinds
Rent dysfunctional garments
So whole me up – subject heaps dislike heaps

Discourse a sort of hat trick
This 1/128th – doubles back – 1/128th – to hungry difference

To thing me more than I
it things me more than it thinks
that is, which express motto is this

Engraved, a stone says:

"This motto all in one I do express.

He was a father to the fatherless."

Skill Saw

Monstrous circles to the right. Don't laugh at the bear in my mind, scratching its head off. How failure describes one's groove as yesterday steps back into the remove.

Chill of dark green. The twilight now spent. Water a blaze within – confined or on hold. Vertical drop beside enormous rocks. No longer the person, but a person's person. Who can as a friend see far. A beauty spot at 100 feet.

Vision crowds a projection of flesh into the tiniest typeface. Legs horned up into a demonstration against. When clowns limp in, it's as if gold becomes an iridescence. Proof that style can liberate itself. A subtraction embraced or contaminated.

Beyond politics, proper nouns abide the stylus release. Ankle to ankle – no shield of time gone. Behind one's back, skin is composed or impelled. Shoes laced, ligaments pounding.

Thesis: if "we" exists, it was guilty before. Please pull to pause. As the berry men picked at a desolate bush, Wyoming was merely a state – a roadside or a verb. Gerund of questionable pause.

2.2

King Code

Written keys a variable
taking lunch or
                              fingertips, regrettably

To imagine hard to imagine
Its boiled wool cloaks me
each on a raised platform

Parroting the spelled incorrect
dictation or birdlife –
               confined by talk or by a word

twisting into an ear
It is a striking almost control
but in that almost, some of the most

delicious nouns whose deviant stands
betray adjustment
I equals OPEN paren APOSTROPHE

S quote NEGATIVE selection CLOSE quote.
Only the worst digressions – modular
preambles – sigh – on a dotty line

Down at the pixel grill the menu is all show
a pop-up of refreshed rates
lost in the client code

To set talk on – the memory variable
we read that's a negative or inverted date (british period)
to dictate the count whose variance I own

Control plus Alt: that text pads through
the pictured host too prompt to
partition what winks behind checkered masks

An expression as an invalid clause the
tools threaten to enfold
Click here to save now

Logic's net – a formula
or flaw that writes 'never enough'
on blackboard walls

The imperial voice barks
back – majestic force to launch
the lord's don

whose royal vice
grips the application creep
        in your wild eyes

Descriptionary: the scene of writing

I joined the frieze to which I
was formerly glazed. But waiting to be
breathed on – one only pretends pottery rules

Pursuit is an opposite pole
to seize the commas when I interrupts
Appearance
severed from the model that deforms it

They spit out their book-to-come as if to prove
my absence

Have you seen this word 'flame'
            that bends to a likeness
in the obscure or impersonal flats – the page
a recycled economy of groans
words live with – a vocabulary of so much
wish fulfillment

            The white-out a storm
            until an eyepatch of color – chameleon
            whose tongue is longer than any-body

This is addressed to Mister Anonymous & Active
Mr. You-Are-Something-But-Nothing or vice versa

First, I left my face at the door & locked in
then, like a Puritan flower, I kept my mouth shut

> Infested digs the hearts cushion
> I might think by representational 'cleaning up'
> how a pronounced fist underscores
> but skin first & all – a veneer too
> difficult as sentences pile up

ii.

Thus, Democritus was the cutest of the ancient critics
swollen with [illegible] but failing
            the true / false test on Aristotle

Dear Professor White:

I can't stand what the pen sets out, no more
greater than – less than – signs

That is my equal – a negative
mirror too close   in the toy shop of
taste – where one moment of bliss
            follows – the icing I'd wished for
            in an easy chair

iii.

A man is all adjectives, floral
patterns after a ball.

She fashioned the monad around his throat.
Nothing is more swallowed – morning's
digressions – leveling until one says 'whenever'

Presiding over the drink
    which after a national
phrase as base is large.

Organized on the basis of whether hunger can wait
    trucks lost in the ratio to roads
In real terms, there is no common
sense.

    Anything is allowable as long as it is
extravagant enough.

The procedural cold stops – a running
fiction. Inherent till it hurts – or until waste
        becomes me.

Calling all theories – is this operating plan

too personal?

With unlimited

time, he put his money

in his mouth.

iv.

-after C.

What to think when no one objects?
Downsized, an echo is unteachable
wherever errant singularity resides.

Uncompromised, he runs over cats
& dogs to get
                    to doorways in which

speech. A dialogue is voiced just in time
but few enter the race whose theory
thrills against itself.
                    Building character,
the difficulties mime themselves, but never
reproduce. Drawing finger to wound,
a man forgets the error whose word-
bursts surround him.
                    A circle's halo corrects,
proving three heads are better – or equal to
the nine noses words trace as analogies for air.

Opening a door I am weaker
back braced, a sentence now complete.

Reluctance submits: paper balloons.

'A' vanishes at point 'the'

                                        What flowers – in

the head of he who knows

how many sheep he has? Call

this a standard if living, a shadow

if pushing into the outline of sleep

        until a convention

        provokes

the form's denouement.

v.

"Transcendence, despite its best efforts, is a mode of becoming immanent".

-Brian Mazzumi

Suspenders – tied to a voice
of what joy isn't – green
bellies of lawn – the dissolve of
careful bricks into baroque columns

As brevity awards someone's figment
one goes unilateral in the affirmative 'and'
words
translate against you
to enter the reliability fault – until
there is no what
divided by how against this
kind of received experience

where justified meaning means justified

It's the dysfunctional equivalent – an
unenhanced association of norms

vi.

Continuity is the foundation upon which discontinuity is institutionalized

An actual badland
eroded point of the body's orbit

light through which the moon
                    dwarf a million
                    times that of water

frozen
how faster a point can

          with the hands
          she kicked it
into a rectangular area
in front of the net

In [*your city here*] no rhyme nor
          reason blisters. If the trip is worth it
memory (the wind) attacks

It is just one of those things –
          it-ness – until the fat groans off
Ground into intervals, there are

limited visiting hours

Pedestrians have arrived but
        don’t let them in – this is
the bookshop
where books are not for sale

C's Relation To O (after Goya)

Smirk of the fervent crescent
Running out of legs

My blemish, white mountain
to modernism – only flesh
has an eye whose blood shot
through, whose fix straps off
the word extinct in waves of red

✲

Continuity longs to crawl its
crippled walk to rail or jump
          until a body not as steep
equal to a slope
a person resembles – what I climb
          as smoke answers
a call of fenced muscles, a
          signal whose disjuncts mount
till most possessed
          fingers adjust the web
that fiction wings

Crime (A): touch the wire 'and'

It was an external stall
mobs of rope
          to hammock us yellow

with heat – a hand shaker's pipe
poor apology for a window
          vast airless or innocent cot

          the lights   but light
and the worst   no worse
if imagination attend them

Alien Exotica

Whose dim wit speaks
beyond or apart where I think

beyond the national slur, where
poetry longs for its box

that shell where the tongue
branded red

unhands the sun – a pain
seeking out – displaced white

frozen loops of the broken plate
whose magic – repeating these last words

    "a round of dirt baked white"

reaches up, into the tumble of error

But doing its flame thing
    who cares to
    handle the wayward squash
who roots for a chair
to seek the night's compassion

Text To Go

-for Mr. Megaphone

Men [sic] can see nothing around them that is not their own image; everything speaks to them of themselves. Their very landscape is alive.

–K. Marx

Unnatural, diminished in itself, X is the spot I can't stand. Confused I thought my hat, my heart, my hybrid.

Anywhere but here where I connects. It's a functional apparatus that captures steamy black and whites, extended phrases lost in some programmed language. I is at pains to resist every lateral, the relations that urge us – students of power – not to profess.

Blue as harsh reminder of forgotten bruises. Open in the time it has now lost, X dreams of a sentence unmatched at every stop. Within the busy signal, metaphor becomes illness. Anxiety in velvet – the wall of worry proves we stand untopped – groveling in the dark. An infrared song whose I sits X'd out. A grid of internal feedback plugging some grim leak. But it isn't a simple spill. There are too many words, too many dot dot dots.

Disinhibitors suppress the anti-urge and celebrate the tenuous lift of the eternal negative. The double whammy of compound returns.

Ouch, I says. As fruit multiplier, a sincere economy baked flat – the jig's up – no more trickle down. Gravitas until the head heels over. X mis-takes hope as desire for the improper this. That that was or wouldn't be. The forever told.

Starting on the wrong page, it was a hoax. An inverted ox says hi, but remains the same. Dead letters that refuse reflection. I is an I or isn't. X becomes something to stand under. A trellis hosting the prehensile I whose greedy wisteria – handcuffed in the mould of time – tends not to remember. It's ok, thinks X. I entered the institute, an inscrutable apparatus with limitless appointments. Awaiting industrial output, the skin dusted or touched up. Untended for redress.

What is the half life of I and I? Biologically pointless the two intersect and molt contradictions. A rose refuses to shed its petals. Slow down! X interlineates while I exerts its verticality. They grow apart but not yet. They swear one word at a time, and shake hands whenever I is present to do the feeling.

As a negative, I leads to blank affect. Precious word that befalls the winter – X as a form of resist.

When insubordination is the healthiest symptom anything becomes a euphemism for denial of responsibility. X disagrees. Guilt is externalized, and thus demonstrates a lack of imagination.

A triangle of outraged fact, chance conserves each habit. It's already happened. The apex of co-option reads as a parable of liberty. I raced to trademark the quickest path to egalité fraternité...

X reads to find something tragic as I rewrites X's *idea of comedy*. Why do they call them routines? Count the habits that hold it there. Is no joke enough? What is so routine, squatting to own the little earth? Is the square foot beneath us finally so tragic?

2.3

Value Unmapped

From the assembly line to the command line

"How do you feel now?"

-The Verizon Guise

This has become the question. There's a need to constantly check the power of connection. It's a visceral gratification of limitless reach. I don't so much hear you as I feel a connection or I don't. After Reagan this is all that matters in politics, at least most of the time. In a sort of reverse short hand, the culture reads only gestures – the emoticons, the semaphores of videoclips, soundbytes that sidle into perception with an immediate sheen. If there's a lesson to be learned, it's that I really do need to sound more like Lorne Greene. Power is transmitted one word at a time and diction is more efficacious than content. Already, you're either with me or against me – eyes diverting to another page.

Without Struggle

an aggregate of follicles
palmately lobed, blue or white flowers
poisonous in both senses
tuberous root – no dust

The alternative is quantity not quality. Not a form that answers the question of function. That is, not a form, but a formlessness that cannot be denied.

So it's not extension that dominates but confrontation. Form is no longer just an extension of content or vice versa.

The problems are precious. If we could only eliminate the need to embrace a single variant. A product instantly pushed through development to release.

Something is lost or confused as one moves station to workstation.

This essay is on the lookout for Motor City hooks, for a sort of urban concrete that can be our pillow, reinforcing a need to walk both into and on the landscape. The felt cushions of suburbia push back – holding up or capturing the body's nostalgia. Oh for that lost rump roast. It's curtains again for the content that moves you – demanding a divorce of the same.

We must consider that Motown remains the negative model for all city planners, which makes Detroit the key to many maps. The resounding bribe becomes the bride of repetition. The recurrence of sports stadia provides the back beat that pounds in after it stops *going on.*

Storm drain.

Harmonics are heard in the body with an affect that easily carries it away. But as the affect draws me towards the center of the city, the text simultaneously pushes me to its margins. At 8 mile, the threshold, the jambs aren't so much kicked out as they are both inside out and outside in.

Help is delivered up-tempo. Happiness is a dirge, an adornment for millions.

These speculations are tentative. But me, I've already lost my place, a place which says nothing. White noise forms negative space all around us. Urban landlock in the narrows. The fishkill a park.

I saw you at the stop and pray, a temple built to Morse comma Samuel. The guy who dashed and dotted – fingers snapping in synch with his head – so that our mouths rope off whatever miswired thought. Your job here to read what's lost in transmission, what's caught in the mud flaps.

Too soft to play, the city is a herd of others. Down to their socks, the birds call out a sequence of contradictions. Crow with metal anklets – yellow with white or red stripes. This identifies the citizen but also directs a mode of expression. We are both the many and the nonce.

Exemplars of becoming what.

We read only the gesture of what is in the air. Which makes these lonely gestures. Always looking – as if singularities could act together, a coincidence expressed.

Did I say my proposed title seeks no map? It finds itself beyond the river of many boats. An impulse stream in a dry bed. The new revolution like a man on a treadmill, disembodied in itself. Its simulation is its truth.

As conveyer belts brought the jobs to the worker and compartmentalized time and space, we lived in fear of becoming that. In relation to an expression we've already become.

In the infrastructure of this dead space we are exposed. A sort of triumph of the orphans – towering objects await their old vertigo. An overwhelming memory of past mistakes. Physical memory abandoned in monumental form. The precious cracks in my façade, ointment creased in the deprived run-off. The cladding taunt – all ooze and muck.

Waiting for the gentry to return, living their biologically appointed lives, the neighbors bide their time.

The direction would be to show what's inside. But that means sutures, and one prefers smooth space where a soft stain is on and of the world. Blistered skin of the head cook – our new state quarter. French straits narrowed as the water drives into view.

The boulevards are now clear for the transit that regulates growth.

How to infuse the mystery? How to place one's story into what – a sodality of constraints? Each as many, a part played, one transparent mask over another. Scotch tape as mask medium – distortion my ass – it's our translucent ornament to worn flesh.

Committees formed for more naming.

Without a map should not imply pursuit of one. If you've found yourself here, this is a success.

It started in large public corporations and appeared to unite labor and capital. But as Orwell suggests, some capital is more equal. The reality of a market democracy is exactly that some dollars are more equal than yours.

Cranked up under a spent hood, an engine winks. Cerise flower rising late in pursuit of the sun's adjustable rate.

The apparatus and its functionaries are in place. If there is time, it becomes a useful prosthesis to the culture. After all, the chorus is here to stay, to sing.

There's no time to be brief. Condensation is a group effort. Like a blind spot for authority each superstition presumes the unseen will ultimately seek you out. As if value were a simple register – misplaced whenever forgetting is in ascent.

It's a short walk through the cake. Almost a feedback loop to those sharpening their knives. Don't be fooled by the appearance of prose – that boat is in the bottle and will stay there. Forced into serial form, time was disqualified and broken into quantified segments, modular engines that debase labor. Meanwhile capital relaxes, untaxed.

Mr. Taylor eyed the world and saw packets, byte-sized tasks. Like economies of scale, divisions of labor appeared to have few restrictions. With M's law we're falling toward the black hole – futures or false dystopias of pure connection. Z's arrow finally pinned up on the board – its trajectory fixed, its mystery lost.

After Marx, we need to own our own prosthetic relation to these machines. This is the new property question. Once the prosthetic is no longer other, the potential is there for it to ventriloquise us. The question becomes whether it will have anything for us to say.

A baby grows to own its hands, its head, its heart.

Like the little engine that couldn't, I embraced a word until it became mine, but then it was lost. Feeling after Creeley, like – life – like, like an unnatural or craven beast – suspended or unfinished.

Against the spoken word, the written word folk call their all-encompassing program language. It is an unstutterable song.

Labor's pathetic last. A leverage of the common, the alienation which is now made dynamic. No longer binary. That is, we now worship or desire our own abstraction.

Chapter: we're apparatchiks or we're nothing.

The concretion is a time polished stone. Try to grasp its trajectory as it hits the circled outcast. Drunk or stumbling into a spontaneous barrage. The shock of pinched recoil – youth of stacked stone – this water dam of work is what we worders want – organized to get – sticks and stones.

The super is all hardware, concrete and glass. It stands against a soft or unsculpted forest. Demarcations are made by an army of functionaries that uphold an apparatus, a construct that sets loose innumerable applications.

Within is as soft. Indescribable, the adjective flows to coalesce. Throwing bodies at it, occupation unknown. The deformities are fungible. A hand hears what the eyes touch.

Infra – or what holds us back also holds us up. The spine she is a wondrous thing. Edging the lawn, I proceeded to build a computer of stones – counting blooms, an inventory of bulbs. Reading surface, the bird's eye meets an expanse of skin. Glide as then a motion towards a common surface. As the ball hits a glove, the celebration of any object. The language as a game is soft – life regulated within its lines.

Paid to forget, I recall more. Hijacked by the text a suspension bridge flanked the city and hovered, assessing the maze. In pursuit of delegable tasks – the one-offs fall up. Doing time to fill the space.

Yes. How do you feel now? The piecework of ruined hands. Every theory abandoned.

Once upon a time labor lacked the power to be affected by anything other than its old self-interest. The future as compensation. The bonus always a bribe.

But now shareholder value has become the sublime. Beyond words, the value is no longer tangible. Merely a deficit in the wake of the worship of some moment presumed essential. The privatization of the past.

How we intuit our inherited place.

In response, Labor married Intellect and divorced Politics, rejecting the adage that 3's company, 2's a crowd. Politics is left alone to form its own stultifying mass. Molar rather than fluid, it resists flows rather than joining and subverting. Absorbs singularities rather than breeding them. But this is perhaps the job of the city – overseeing innumerable mergers into singular lines. The patient plow of modernity stirs seed into soil, sowing the perverse that makes us human.

Afterword.

The simple register misplaced whenever forgetting is in ascent. It's a short walk home. The body wants to forget – but becomes a victim of the involuntary. It collects itself as it falls, tumbling forward.

Proprioception of the dash – a pause longer than a comma and less than a full stop. Don't be fooled by the appearance of prose – something lurks in the pudding. Remember how the boat in the bottle stays there.

It's a mystery or betrayal, where stasis partners with the virtual. Instinct remains a control – as if it were a preserve of the actual, an internalized contradiction.

Marriage is a machine that talks back – but its revolution was too late. Each song boils down to one phrase. An algorithm that forced value into serial form. As if it simply harnessed a blind spot for authority.

No, he is the unstoppable author, the Stephen Spielberg of structural engineering.
No, we can only pray for failure.
Yes, time is deserted in quantified segments – in the modular engines that debase labor.

Thesis: We need to own our own prosthetics. My hand in relation.

The machine was No's other lover
What was once conveyed is now lost
At the innovation station locusts lift the landscape
A network of exemplars abandoned the family store
Urban planning as fear of Detroit

OK. Take a brief look at the star structure. A face emerges from the assembly line. Neither materially grounded nor aloft. What a beautiful ass it has. Forget you.

Labor produces its own aliens. For example, the Pinkertons were agoraphobes who voted against themselves. Trenchcoat libertarians adrift in the flows of capital.

The urge is to worship our own abstraction from labor. Just wait for the return of lotto tickets, the next round of unfiltered cigarettes. Realizing the body's capacity to absorb even more savage value, I took my daily constitutional. Prozac and a single malt.

Sentences because to get inside beneath attention's filter, one must build a kinescope that holds the scene together, where the viewer enters lost in wonder as the whiplash of thought carries it to the end.

Wax World is being completed as the first Chax Press book of 2011, the twenty-eighth year of operation for the press, 25 of which have found us in Tucson, Arizona.

Centaur, designed by Bruce Rogers, is the text type for the book. Fonts used for titling are Gill Sans and Lithos. Design of the book has been in the capable hands of Lynn Thompson. The cover image is by Gary Hill.

Chax Press is a 501(c)(3) nonprofit organization that has published more than 120 books, including fine art editions and trade editions of literature and book art works.

For more information, please see our web site at http://chax.org

Chax Press is supported by individual contributions, and in part by the Tucson Pima Art Council and the Arizona Commission on the Arts, with funds from the State of Arizona and from the National Endowment for the Arts.

TUCSON PIMA ARTS COUNCIL

Arizona Commission on the Arts

NATIONAL ENDOWMENT FOR THE ARTS